2025 is a Shhh Show
The Struggles in Today's Job Market

2025 is a Shhh Show

The Struggles in Today's Job Market

By Char Vernon

Copyright Page

2025 is a Shhh Show - The Struggles in Today's Job Market
Copyright © 2025 by Char Vernon

> The information in this book is based on the author's experience and research. It is provided for informational purposes only and should not be considered legal or financial advice. Readers are encouraged to consult a qualified professional regarding specific workplace situations.

First Edition
Published by: Char Vernon
Website: www.visionaryconsults.org

✉ For permissions, media inquiries, or bulk orders, contact: info@visionaryconsults.org

Dedication

To the federal government employees who were silenced, sidelined, or swept out of service, this is for you.

To those who lost their jobs, and to those who felt the only option left was to take the Deferred Resignation Program, I want you to know that your dedication, your expertise, and your impact did not go unnoticed.

You gave your time, your energy, your loyalty, and often your peace of mind in service to a system that didn't protect you when it mattered most.

This book is a reflection of your reality, a record of our shared frustration, and a reminder that you were never alone in this fight.

— Char Vernon

Preface

Let's skip the corporate fluff, 2025 is a mess.

If you picked up this book, you're probably exhausted, frustrated, and wondering how the hell we got here. You've applied for dozens, maybe hundreds of jobs, only to be ghosted by roles that pay less than your last rent increase. You have the degrees, the experience, and the work ethic, yet you're constantly told you're either "overqualified" or somehow not quite the right fit.

The job market today is a paradox. Employers are begging for talent while simultaneously rejecting it. Automated systems judge your worth before a human ever lays eyes on your name. Interviews feel more like performance art than an actual assessment of skill. And if you're lucky enough to land something, there's a good chance the pay is insulting and the expectations are delusional.

This book is not a motivational speech wrapped in buzzwords. It's not going to tell you to "manifest" your way into a corner office or "network harder" at events that feel like speed dating with people who don't remember your name. What you will find here is the truth, the real, unfiltered, and sometimes ugly side of navigating today's job market.

You'll find stories, satire, and uncomfortable honesty. You'll laugh, you'll nod, and maybe you'll cry. But most importantly, you'll know you're not alone in this chaos. You're not crazy. The system is.

This book is for the job seekers, the laid off, the overworked, the underpaid, and the ones who are just trying to keep their head above water in a system designed to drown them.

Welcome to the shit show.

Acknowledgments

First, I would like to thank the United States federal government for making this book possible by pushing me, and thousands of others, out the door with the Deferred Resignation Program. Your chaos gave me content.

To the HR professionals and recruiters who ghosted me, strung me along for six rounds of interviews, or offered me salaries that could not even cover a week of groceries, thank you. You helped shape entire chapters.

To my friends who listened to me rant, spiral, regroup, and then repeat the cycle, you are appreciated more than you know.

To the readers, especially those struggling through this job market, this book is for you. You are not crazy, you are not alone, and you are certainly not imagining how broken the system is.

And finally, to my former coworkers, the real ones, you know who you are. Your work ethic, humor, and humanity inspired me to keep going when I wanted to quit.

We may not have walked out the front door with applause, but we left with our dignity, our stories, and now, our receipts.

— Char Vernon

Table Contents

INTRODUCTION: Welcome to the Circus. You're the Clown

Congratulations! You've just entered the 2025 job market... a place where hope goes to die, resumes get ghosted, and "competitive pay" means they'll pay you in exposure, anxiety, or maybe vibes. If you're reading this, chances are you've either just gotten laid off, applied to 327 jobs with no callback, or stared into the void of LinkedIn until the void started staring back.

This isn't your standard motivational, "You got this!" career guide. Nah. This is for the real ones, the fed-up professionals, the resume warriors, the overqualified "assets" who somehow still can't get a damn interview. You've got the degrees, the certifications, the trauma, and still, you're being told you're not a "culture fit."

In this book, we're gonna talk about all of it: the lies in job descriptions, the theater of panel interviews, the government's disappearing act, and how AI thinks "team player" is more important than 10 years of experience. You're not crazy. The system is.

So pour a drink. Light a candle. Cry a little if you need to. This book is part rant, part therapy, part resource, and all truth.

Let's get into this sh*t show, shall we?

CHAPTER 1

You Don't Speak ATS, You Don't Exist

CHAPTER 1: If You Don't Speak ATS, You Don't Exist

Once upon a time, you could walk into a business, hand someone your resume, and possibly land a job. Fast forward to 2025, and if your resume doesn't say "synergize," "cross-functional," or "proven track record" at least twelve times, it's going straight into a digital dumpster fire.

Welcome to the world of Applicant Tracking Systems (ATS) software designed to help companies filter applicants but secretly created by Satan himself (probably in collaboration with LinkedIn's evil twin). ATS doesn't care that you managed a team of 20, implemented cost-saving processes, or survived three toxic bosses. If your resume doesn't match the exact wording of the job post, you're invisible.

It's like playing resume Bingo... but the recruiter is holding the card upside down and blindfolded.

You:

"Led multiple cross-departmental initiatives using Agile methodologies."

Job description:

"Seeking candidate who managed various interdepartmental projects with Scrum framework."

ATS:

"No match. Reject."

Excuse me?!

So here's what you do: You become a resume contortionist. You tailor each one like you're customizing a suit for a fussy fashion designer. It doesn't matter if you've done the work. You have to phrase it in their words, in their tone, and pray the system doesn't choke on your creativity.

We've gone from storytelling our careers to keyword-stuffing like SEO addicts on Red Bull. Want to show that you're a visionary leader? Too bad. The robot only recognizes "supervised." Want to say you're an innovative strategist? Nope. Try "analyzed data and implemented procedures."

Forget being authentic. Be algorithmic.

Because in 2025, you're not trying to impress a person... you're trying to win a robot's attention in a Hunger Games-style application war. And even if you win? Congrats. You've just been invited to your first of five interviews, one of which includes a pop quiz and a "team vibe check."

Godspeed.

JOB SEEKER BINGO

How close to the edge are you?

B	I	N	G	O
Got ghosted	Took a mental health nap	Rewrote resume again	Applied to a job with no salary listed	Got "we went in another direction" email
Referred by a friend	Interviewed with 4+ people	Asked to do a free assignment	Didn't hear back at all	Salary was insulting
Posted "Open to Work"	Cry-scrolled LinkedIn	Was told you're overqualified	Applied out of spite	Saw your dream job reposted
took a break to cry	Pretended to be "excited"	Was asked about your 5-year plan	Said "I love your mission"	Forgot what jog you applied for
Practiced STAR answers	Stalked interviewer on LinkedIn	Took an unpaid skills test	Got called the wrong name	Wrote another damn cover letter

5 in a row = You've unlocked chaos mode. Go eat a cookie.

CHAPTER 2

You're Too Good. We're Going with Someone... Meh

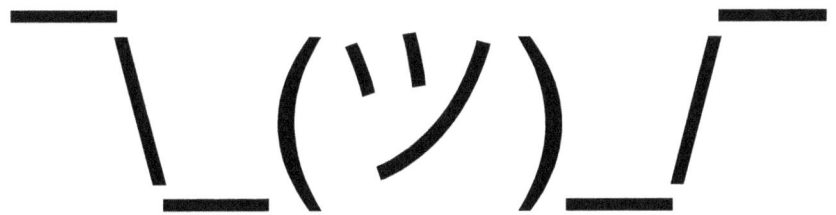

CHAPTER 2: You're Too Good. We're Going with Someone... Meh

You crushed the application. You had the experience, the confidence, and even managed to spell "liaison" correctly without autocorrect. You nailed the interview. You smiled through your teeth, made eye contact like a psycho, and said "I'm passionate about stakeholder engagement" with a straight face.

But then... you get the email:

"Thank you for your interest. While we were impressed by your qualifications, we have decided to move forward with other candidates whose experience more closely aligns with our needs."

Translation:

"You're overqualified and we don't know what to do with you, so we're going with someone cheaper, less experienced, and more willing to be gaslit into thinking this is a 'growth opportunity.'"

Let's be clear: being overqualified should never be a dealbreaker. That's like saying, "You're too skilled to do this job well, so we're passing." It's corporate doublespeak for "We're scared you'll leave the moment you realize this job sucks" or worse, "You intimidate the manager who's been coasting for 12 years."

They don't want a rockstar. They want a tambourine player who follows orders and doesn't ask for a raise.

In 2025, "overqualified" is the scarlet letter. It's what they say when you've got degrees, certifications, war stories, and receipts, but they'd rather hire someone who needs three weeks of onboarding just to figure out how to set up their Outlook calendar.

You don't get brownie points for being a high performer anymore. You get blacklisted.

And let's talk about the real kicker... these same companies that ghosted you for being too much will turn around and whine that "no one wants to work anymore." Really? People want to work, you just want workers who will accept low pay, high stress, zero boundaries, and a "family culture" that feels like a hostage situation.

You're not too good for the job. The job is too insecure to handle your excellence.

CHAPTER 3

Looking for a Unicorn with Minimum Wage Expectations

CHAPTER 3: Looking for a Unicorn with Minimum Wage Expectations

Ah yes, the job posting. A modern work of fiction.

Let's dissect a typical 2025 job ad:

We're seeking a self-starter with 10 years of experience, a master's degree, emotional intelligence, expert-level Excel skills, fluency in Mandarin, project management certification, and the ability to juggle flaming swords on TikTok while optimizing ROI. Compensation: $42,000/year and a Pizza Friday once a quarter.

Who's writing these descriptions? Willy Wonka on a budget?

Somewhere along the line, job descriptions turned into corporate wishlists. It's not even about finding the right person anymore. It's about shooting for the stars while offering gas station wages. You want an IT specialist who can also do your admin work, run HR, train your dog, and plan your company retreat, and you want them to do it for less than it costs to rent a studio apartment near your office. Bold.

Let's not forget the unnecessary hoops:

- Upload your resume, then re-type every single thing line-by-line into the system.

- Attach a cover letter that no human will read.
- Take a 40-minute personality quiz that determines whether you're too much of an introvert to process invoices.

And then... silence. Or worse, a rejection before your coffee gets cold.

They want the perfect candidate. Someone who:

- Doesn't need training
- Will stay forever
- Will never ask for a raise
- Doesn't have "childcare obligations" (yes, that's code)
- Won't challenge authority, policy, or the outdated office dress code from 2002

The job market today is the equivalent of showing up to a pawn shop with a diamond, only to be offered a Happy Meal in return.

So, if you're sitting there thinking, "Is it me?" nah. It's them.

CHAPTER 4

You're Hired! Just Kidding. We've Ghosted You

CHAPTER 4: You're Hired! Just Kidding. We've Ghosted You

Job hunting in 2025 is like dating someone with a burner phone and commitment issues. You apply. You wait. You get the call. You're excited. You show up looking sharp, wearing that fake "I totally slept last night" smile. You go through three interviews, a skills test, and even a personality assessment that basically asked if you'd snitch on a coworker for stealing lunch.

And then...

Nothing.

No rejection. No follow-up. No "Thanks but no thanks." Just vibes.

The company?
They've moved on.

You?
Still refreshing your inbox like it owes you money.

Let's be clear: ghosting isn't a glitch, it's policy now. HR departments and recruiters will "circle back" so many times, you'd think they're training for the Olympics. The truth is, they filled the job internally, or decided to "reassess their needs," or hired someone's cousin's girlfriend's dog walker. But they'll never say that. That would be professional.

Instead, you're left in emotional limbo. Did they hate me? Was I too confident? Not confident enough? Should I have used a different background on Zoom? (Spoiler: it wasn't the virtual plant wall.)

And don't even get me started on the ones who make you jump through hoops like:

- "We'd love for you to put together a 12-slide strategic marketing pitch."
- "Submit a writing sample outlining a full HR onboarding process with flowcharts."
- "Take this 90-minute unpaid assessment to show us you're serious."

Serious? SERIOUS? Baby, I was serious before I skipped lunch to fill out your glitchy application portal and uploaded the same resume in three different file formats.

Ghosting is the corporate way of saying: "We never saw you as human in the first place." Because if they did, they'd do what grown people do: communicate.

So, dear job seeker: If they ghosted you, take it as a favor. They've shown you their respect level before you ever signed on the dotted line.

Let the trash take itself out.

CHAPTER 5

Depressed? Anxious? Broke? Congrats, you're in the Club

CHAPTER 5: Depressed? Anxious? Broke? Congrats, you're in the Club

Let's talk about the stuff that doesn't make it onto LinkedIn:
- ✓ The crushing anxiety.
- ✓ The sleepless nights.
- ✓ The "do I even matter?" spiral you get into after the fifth rejection in one week... for jobs you could do with your eyes closed.

And let's not forget the new favorite hobby of the unemployed: staring at your phone waiting for an interview request that never comes while simultaneously talking yourself out of a panic attack.

In case no one's said it: job searching is a mental health crisis. It's not "fun employment." It's psychological warfare disguised as a productivity challenge.

They tell you to "stay positive."

You: I've eaten four granola bars and cried in the shower twice today, but sure, I'll stay positive.

The gaslighting is real.

The toxic positivity is louder than ever:
"Everything happens for a reason."
"Use this time to rebrand yourself!"

"This is an opportunity for growth."

Miss me with all that.
Growth? Sis, I'm trying to keep the lights on.

Let's break it down:

- Anxiety: The kind that makes you feel guilty for not applying to 10 jobs before 10 a.m. every morning, even though you're emotionally running on fumes.
- Depression: That fun little voice that shows up around 2 p.m. every day whispering, "You'll never get hired again."
- Imposter Syndrome: Despite having years of receipts and credentials, you start questioning if you're even good at anything. (Cue flashbacks to the one time you forgot to unmute during a Zoom meeting.)
- Burnout: Oh, you thought burnout only came from working? Nah. Turns out you can burn out from trying to work and constantly being told you're not enough.

Meanwhile...

You're still expected to smile through it.
Still expected to show up to interviews chipper and well-groomed.

Still expected to write perky cover letters that scream, "I am passionate about your mission!"
(Even though your real passion is not crying in the breakroom of a retail job at 49.)

We're walking resumes with bills. That's what it feels like. But here's what they don't tell you: this isn't your fault.

You're not lazy.
You're not broken.
You're not "not trying hard enough."
You're in a rigged system that's designed to exhaust you into submission.

So what now?

Do what you gotta do. Nap unapologetically.
Apply to one job a day and call it a win.
Block "motivational speakers" who suggest waking up at 4 a.m. to journal your way to success.
Eat your comfort food and don't you dare feel guilty about it.

Because in 2025, surviving the job hunt is an achievement. And if no one's told you yet?

You're doing great, even if you feel like sh*t.

Sidebar: Real Talk Mental Health Tips (That Don't Involve Buying a $12 Smoothie)

1. Set job search hours.
   You're not a machine. Treat the job hunt like a job but with set hours. 9–12 = applications. After that You're off the clock.

2. Create a 'Win List.'
    Not hired? Still winning. Made a new resume version? Win. Didn't throw your laptop out the window today? Big win.
3. Journal the rage.
    Get a notebook. Title it: "You Can't Say This in a Cover Letter." Use it.
4. Unfollow the "Success Gurus."
    If Chase is out here saying "just manifest harder," block him. Chase owns a boat from his trust fund. You're built different.
5. Move your body.
    Not for weight loss. Not for "discipline." Just to remind yourself you exist outside of job boards and rejection emails.
6. Have something daily that isn't tied to money.
    Paint, walk, read, scream into a pillow, anything that doesn't remind you of bills.

Insert: Fictional HR Rejection Letter #1 – The "Too Awesome" Version

Dear Applicant,

Thank you for your interest in our position. While your qualifications, experience, and glowing aura are undeniably impressive, we've decided to move forward with a candidate who better fits our... vague vibes.

In truth, your competence terrifies us, and we worry you'll realize we're disorganized, underpaying, and still using Windows 7.

Best of luck, and please don't sue us.

Sincerely,

The People Who Will Regret This
Job Search Self-Care Checklist (No Toxic Positivity Allowed)

- ☑ Ate something that wasn't instant noodles
- ☑ Didn't compare yourself to that annoying person who just "landed a six-figure remote role with no degree"
- ☑ Cried once (but not more than three times)
- ☑ Rewrote your resume for the 14th time with a new font because maybe this time...
- ☑ Watched trash TV guilt-free
- ☑ Texted someone, "Why is job hunting like this?" and they said, "Same."
- ☑ Closed LinkedIn before 9 p.m. (or ever)
- ☑ Didn't throw phone at wall during a rejection email
- ☑ Showed up. That's enough.

CHAPTER 6

Pay Cut? That's Not a Cut, That's Amputation

CHAPTER 6: Pay Cut? That's Not a Cut, That's Amputation

In this economy, when they say "you may have to take a pay cut," what they really mean is:

"We'd love for you to do what you've always done, just for significantly less. And be grateful about it."

Cut?

Babe, they're asking for a financial lobotomy.

Let's say it loud for the people in the back of the unemployment line:

Taking a pay cut does not mean you're worth less. It means employers are trying to finesse the system while still flexing on Instagram about their "record profits."

Real-Life Job Offer Math:

Old Job:
$89,000/year + benefits + remote

New Offer:
$54,000/year + "great team culture" + mandatory office days + no dental

That's not a job offer. That's a polite mugging.

And then they hit you with the emotional manipulation:

"This is a great opportunity to grow!"
"We're a mission-driven organization."
"There's potential for promotion in 3-5 years."

Let me tell you something, you can't pay rent in "potential."

And unless your landlord accepts exposure and positive vibes, that paycheck better show up looking like it has some respect.

The Corporate Logic Breakdown:

Their Expectations	Reality
"You Should be flexible with your salary."	Inflation is disrespecting my life.
"We offer intrinsic rewards"	Translation: broke
"We're like a family"	Dysfunctional, toxic, and unpaid
"We believe in servant leadership."	You're the servant. They are the leader.

And the best part? These are the same jobs you left five years ago, now rebranded with twice the responsibilities and half the salary.

Fun With Fictional Math

- Pre-COVID salary: $75,000
- Post-COVID offer: $52,000
- Rent increase: +22%
- Utilities: +15%
- Eggs: Still $7 for no damn reason
- Bank account: Haunted
- Mental state: "Let me call you right back" forever

Snarky Survival Suggestions:

1. Ask for more. Always.
   If they ghost you for negotiating, it wasn't a job it was a trap.
2. Do the math.
   After taxes, commuting, parking, and the mental cost of waking up early, you might actually be paying them.
3. Keep receipts.
   Screenshot job listings before they disappear. You'll want those when they change the job description halfway through the offer process.
4. Don't let desperation discount your dignity.
   You are not cheap labor. You are expensive talent waiting on someone with actual vision.

Final Thought:
If taking a pay cut feels like betrayal? That's because it is. And you don't have to sugarcoat it with "maybe this is a step back to leap forward."

No. Sometimes it's just a slap in the face with a paycheck attached.

Hold the line. Know your worth, and add tax.

CHAPTER 7

Panel Interviews: Welcome to Your Public Execution

CHAPTER 7: Panel Interviews: Welcome to Your Public Execution

Picture this: You walk into a room (or log into Zoom), and suddenly you're facing six blank stares across a long table (or six badly lit faces in floating boxes). No one smiles. No one blinks. One person's camera isn't working. Another looks like they're live-streaming from the inside of a microwave. And guess what?

They all have questions.

This, my friend, is a panel interview, also known as corporate hazing.

Why Panel Interviews Are Torture:

- You're being judged in real-time by people who haven't agreed on what they want.
- One person will be overly enthusiastic and fake-friendly. The rest look like they're choosing your casket lining.
- They will ask the same question, slightly reworded, to see if you break.
- You're performing like a trained seal while silently wondering if your deodorant is holding up.

And then they hit you with this classic:

"Tell us about a time you failed."

Sure. Let me just emotionally undress in front of six strangers for a job that pays less than what I made before the pandemic. Absolutely. Let me just relive trauma for a job that might not even call me back.

The Hidden Roles on Every Panel:

1. The Timekeeper: Watching the clock like your answer is cutting into lunch.
2. The Over-Achiever: Asks a 3-part question with a 7-minute setup.
3. The Phantom: Hasn't said a word. Will never speak. Could be AI-generated.
4. The HR Rep: Reads from a sheet like they're hosting a hostage video.
5. The Future Boss: Already decided they want their cousin in the role.
6. The Wild Card: Throws in a question like, "If you were a kitchen utensil, what would you be?"

(Answer: A spatula, because I flip under pressure but still keep it together.)

Let's Talk "Energy"
Panel interviews are the Thunderdome of fake professionalism. You're supposed to show:
- Confidence but not arrogance.
- Passion but not desperation.
- Humor but not too much (we don't want to seem unstable).

- Competence but still coachable.
- Leadership but also obedient.
- Be Black, Brown, queer, neurodivergent, but still fit into their "culture."

It's exhausting. You walk away from that call not even knowing your own name anymore.

Survival Tactics (Snark + Strategy)

1. Write everyone's name down immediately.
   Even if you never use them again, it's the only control you'll have.
2. Stall with a compliment.
   "Great question, Sarah. I appreciate the clarity." = buying five seconds to remember what the hell you're doing.
3. Smile like you're not spiraling.
   The game is to look sane while unraveling inside.
4. At the end, ask a question so intelligent they have to Google it later.

Example: "How does your current talent retention strategy align with post-pandemic flexibility demands and DEI accountability?" Boom. Silence.

Final Thought:

Panel interviews don't measure your ability to do the job.

They measure your ability to perform under pressure in a staged arena full of passive-aggressive gladiators. If you survive, congrats, the reward is maybe a second round. Or just... another email that starts with, "Unfortunately..."

Either way, you earned the right to scream into a pillow and eat carbs.

CHAPTER 8

Is My AI Resume Smarter Than Me?

CHAPTER 8: Is My AI Resume Smarter Than Me?

So you spent three hours tweaking your resume, again.

You opened ChatGPT, asked it to "optimize your experience for a senior-level position," and bam, suddenly you've got bullets that say things like:

- Leveraged synergies across cross-functional paradigms to execute value-centric solutions.

What the hell does that even mean?

If you're wondering whether your AI-generated resume is smarter than you... the answer is complicated. Technically? Maybe. Emotionally? Hell no.

Welcome to the Resume Hunger Games

In 2025, job applications are less about your actual talent and more about whether your resume speaks fluent robot. The ATS bots don't want personality. They don't want context. They want formulas:

- Action Verb + Keyword + Measurable Result + Industry Nonsense Example: "Streamlined stakeholder alignment leveraging CRM dashboards across vertical integration."

YOU: "I sent follow-up emails and got sh*t done."
AI: "You optimized cross-channel workflows to enhance client satisfaction metrics by 17%."
Same thing. Just fancier lies.

So, Should You Use AI to Write Your Resume?

Absolutely.
Because the system is dumb, and you've gotta beat it with its own dumbness.

But here's the catch: Don't let AI erase your voice.
AI doesn't know that you calmed down a pissed-off VP in a board meeting. It doesn't know you took over a crumbling project and carried it on your back like a corporate Atlas. It doesn't know how much BS you've survived with grace and a good playlist. So yes, let AI help you sound "professional. "But go back and put your story in it. Because hiring managers may skim the buzzwords… but they remember real.

FAKE AI-GENERATED RESUME BULLET POINTS (That Say Nothing)

- Orchestrated innovative alignment across value-anchored initiatives.
- Activated end-to-end feedback loops within dynamic internal ecosystems.
- Empowered synergistic methodologies to drive upward mobility.

- I answered emails and reminded grown adults to do their jobs

Red Flags from AI Resumes (or Recruiters Who Use Them)

1. You sound like a robot in a TED Talk.
   Tone matters. Don't lose your human edge.
2. You have buzzwords... but no receipts.
   "Strategic thinker" isn't strategic unless you show how you used it.
3. All jobs sound the same.
   "Led a team" in 4 jobs? Spice it up. Nobody leads the same way twice.
4. Your resume is optimized... but not customized.
   You passed the ATS, now what? Will a human care?

Snarky Tip:

Use AI like seasoning, not the whole damn meal. You are not ChatGPT's intern. You are the damn author of your career, and your resume should sound like it.

Final Thought:

If you've ever stared at your resume and thought, "Who is this person?"... you're not alone. You're trying to beat a rigged system with tools that weren't built for nuance, honesty, or burnout.

So take the help, rewrite the parts that sound like a drunk MBA, and send that thing off with confidence.

Because in 2025, the most "qualified" thing about you might be your ability to translate real hustle into robot-friendly BS.

And that, my friend, is a skill.

CHAPTER 9

Tunnel? What Tunnel?

CHAPTER 9: Tunnel? What Tunnel?

You've heard the phrase a thousand times.

"There's light at the end of the tunnel."

But in the 2025 job market?
That "light" might just be a recruiter's ring light as they prepare to tell you:

"We went in another direction."

Let's be honest: the job search has gone from a temporary inconvenience to a full-blown existential lifestyle. And no one tells you how disorienting it is to lose not just your paycheck, but your identity, routine, and sense of purpose, all in the same damn week.

The Phases of Tunnel Syndrome:

1. The Optimistic Hustle Phase

"I'm going to use this time to rebrand, rebuild, and reset. Maybe I'll start a blog! Maybe I'll go to grad school!"
(You even opened a spreadsheet to track applications. Color-coded, baby.)

2. The Realization Phase

"Okay... 41 applications in and not even a rejection email?"

You start to wonder if the hiring manager died or if your resume has been cursed.

3. The Spiral Phase

"Maybe I'm not smart anymore. Maybe I peaked in 2017. Maybe I should open an Etsy store and sell inspirational lint."
This is when you stare at the ceiling and question everything, including capitalism, your major, and your haircut.

4. The Numb Phase

Applications sent: 92
Interviews scheduled: 1
Number of snacks eaten during Zoom calls: Countless
You're now fluent in rejection and emotionally sponsored by apathy.

5. The Micro-Dose of Hope Phase

"Okay, this one looks like a good fit. I have exactly what they want."
...and so the cycle begins again.

Why the Tunnel Feels Endless

- Because you're not just looking for a job, you're trying to get someone to believe in your value without meeting you, knowing you, or paying attention.

- Because you're dealing with gatekeeping algorithms, corporate indecision, and a country where layoffs trend more than job openings.
- Because even the interviews you do get? Half the time they end with "We're putting the role on hold."

Survival Tips When the Tunnel Starts Feeling Like a Coffin:

1. Switch strategies, not standards.
   You can pivot your approach, but don't water yourself down to get hired by a trash company.
2. Say no sometimes.
   If a job feels wrong, disrespectful, or desperate? It is. Pass.
3. Vent often. Vent loud.
   Whether it's a journal, a friend, or a rage-post draft you never send — get it out.
4. Create structure.
   No structure = no sanity. Schedule a time to stop job searching and rejoin the world.
5. Celebrate anything.
   Showered today? Victory. Didn't punch your laptop? Hero.

Affirmation for the Tunnel Dwellers:

"This system is broken, not me. I am not unemployed because I lack value. I am unemployed because a flawed machine can't see it. My worth existed before a paycheck and will exist after one."

Final Thought:

No, you're not imagining it, the tunnel really does feel longer than it used to. But here's the truth: you're not just surviving it... you're documenting it. Every rejection, every silent application, every awkward panel interview is a receipt.

And one day, whether it's your business, your big break, or just the right person seeing your real damn value, the tunnel will end.

And you'll walk out of it smarter, stronger, and possibly with an entire book deal.

1: Before & After AI Resume Edits

Title: "This Is Me... on AI."

Before (Human version)	After (AI-enhanced version)
Handled employee complaints and helped fix workplace drama	Spearheaded conflict resolution initiatives to enhance organizational culture and employee engagement
Ran the office while my manager was out every Friday	Assumed interim leadership responsibilities, overseeing administrative operations and ensuring continuity of business functions
Answered a ridiculous amount of emails and scheduled 800 pointless meetings	Managed cross-functional communication workflows, coordinating high-volume scheduling and executive-level correspondence
Trained the new guy who didn't know how to use a printer	Onboarded and mentored new personnel, facilitating rapid integration into departmental procedures and tech systems

Moral: You did the work. Let AI do the fluff, just don't let it erase your voice.

2: AI-Generated Resume That Probably Got the Job (But Shouldn't Have)

Title: "The Resume of a Corporate Chameleon"

Brent M. Synergy
Chief Pivot Officer, Optimization Enthusiast, Buzzword Wrangler

Summary:

Visionary thought leader with a passion for paradigm-shifting solutions, leveraging holistic frameworks to drive bottom-line impact in ambiguous environments. Adept at pivoting, ideating, and actualizing scalable synergies.

Experience:
- Orchestrated frictionless transformation across B2B verticals
- Integrated actionable feedback loops to enhance omnichannel deliverables
- Fostered high-impact engagement via agile thought partnership

Skills:
- Synergy

- Alignment
- Stakeholder whispering
- KPI manifesting

Awards:
- "Best Use of Jargon" – 2023
- "Most Likely to Say 'Let's Circle Back'" – Twice

References available if you're into pain.

This is what happens when AI writes your resume without supervision. Don't be Brent.

3: Buzzword Blacklist (Use With Caution or Just... Don't)

Title: "Words That Might Get You the Interview... But Also Might Get You Blocked"

X Results-driven
X Go-getter
X Outside the box
X Rockstar
X Ninja
X Thought leader
X Synergy (seriously, stop)
X Self-starter
X Wheelhouse
X Passionate (unless it's followed by tacos)
X Game-changer

✕ Jack of all trades (translation: they underpaid you)
✕ Wear many hats (translation: unpaid therapist, admin, and event planner)

Try these instead:

- Led, improved, resolved, simplified, collaborated, launched, created, organized, mentored, negotiated, streamlined

Speak in receipts, not riddles.

CHAPTER 10

Dear Government: Help?

CHAPTER 10: Dear Government: Help?

A sobering, sarcastic look at how the 2025 administration has offered "resources" for the unemployed in the same way your ex offered "closure."

📊 Flowchart: Should I Apply for This Job?

2025 edition: Because wasting your time is the new full-time job.

How to use:

Read the posting, roll your eyes, and follow the arrows. Spoiler: You're still applying, but now with sarcasm and lowered expectations.

START
⬇
Does the job require 8 years of experience for an "entry-level" role?
 YES → Red flag. Keep going anyway.
 NO → Wow. A miracle. Next question...
⬇
Do they list the salary?
 NO → They're hiding something.
 YES → Is it insulting?
 YES → Laugh, cry, and move on (or apply out of spite).

NO → Mark that unicorn.

↓

Does the company have a reputation for burning people out?

 YES → Do you have a therapist on standby?

 NO → Proceed with cautious optimism.

↓

Is this the third time they've posted this job in 2 months?

 YES → That's turnover, not opportunity.

 NO → Might actually be hiring. Gasp.

↓

Do you meet 100% of the qualifications?

 YES → They'll say you're overqualified.

 NO → Apply anyway. So will Jeffrey from TikTok with a fake MBA.

↓

Is this job in your actual field?

 YES → It's called alignment. Rare. Treat it gently.

 NO → It's called survival. Welcome.

↓

Final question: Does your gut say "RUN"?

 YES → Apply anyway. Regret is part of the process.

 NO → That's suspicious. But go ahead.

↓

OUTCOME:

Apply. Regret. Repeat.

Bonus: Screenshot the listing in case they ghost you and repost it like it never happened.

Spoiler: They left us on read.

Let's set the scene.
You've been laid off.
You did the right thing: filed for unemployment, checked the Department of Labor website, and looked for "resources for displaced workers."

You were expecting guidance, maybe some dignity. What you got was a PDF last updated in 2013, a dead link to a resume workshop at a closed community college, and a chatbot that says "try again later."

In short?

The system failed you. And it's pretending it doesn't know your name.

Where's the Help?

Remember when COVID-era benefits reminded us that fast government aid was possible?

Yeah. Those days are gone.
Now, the message from the 2025 administration feels like:

"We understand your pain. We're forming a bipartisan task force to discuss your suffering sometime next fiscal year."

Meanwhile, you're behind on rent and hoping Dollar Tree hasn't raised their prices again.

What They Offer vs. What You Need:

What's "Available"	What You Actually Need
A workforce portal with broken links	Rent assistance that doesn't involve a 47-step approval process
Career coaching from someone who last updated their resume in 2009	An actual job that pays more than $19/hour
Free resume classes on PowerPoint	Help paying your damn electric bill
A "Virtual Job Fair" featuring jobs you already applied to on Indeed	Childcare so you can show up to the job if you ever get one
A hotline that's "experiencing unusually high call volume"	A human being with answers

What They Don't Say (But You Feel It):

- "You're not unemployed. You're just not trying hard enough."
- "Why don't you just pivot into tech? Everyone's hiring in AI!"
- "Be grateful for the interview, even if it's unpaid."
- "We don't have money for more programs, but we
- did just give $23 million to a goat yoga startup in Utah."

The system isn't just broken, it's distracted.

Insert: "So You Lost Your Job, Good Luck!" (Fake Government Pamphlet)

Page 1: Have you considered reinventing yourself as a small business owner with no funding, support, or healthcare?
Page 2: We suggest staying positive while your credit score tanks!
Page 3: Our best advice: Manifest harder. Or marry rich

(For real help, visit our outdated .gov site that won't load on mobile.)

What You Can Actually Do (Besides Scream):

1. Document everything.
If you're being denied benefits, request appeals.
Screenshot errors. File complaints. These systems bank on you giving up.
2. Tap community resources.
Mutual aid groups, churches, food banks, community organizations, they're often more helpful than federal agencies.
3. Connect with others.
Reddit forums, job seeker support groups, even TikTok sometimes the best survival hacks come from strangers.
4. Vote like your rent depends on it.
Because it actually does.

Final Thought:

The government says help is "on the way."
Cool. Can it pay a bill now?

Until then, you're on your own, but not alone.
The system wasn't built for you, but you're still standing.
And somehow, in spite of all the bullsh*t, you're still
showing up.

That's power they can't regulate.

CHAPTER 11

What Should I Do About My Bills?

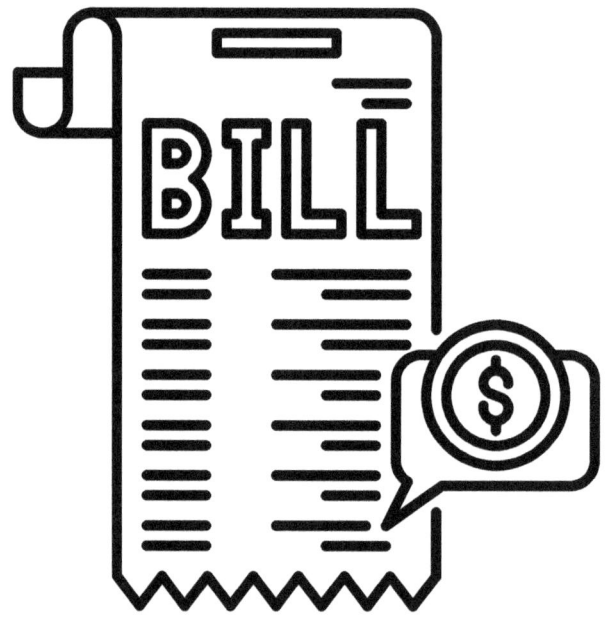

CHAPTER 11: What Should I Do About My Bills?

Budgeting Roulette - 2025 Edition

"What Can I Actually Afford This Month?"

Welcome to the only game where everyone's broke, and the prize is surviving one more billing cycle.

Spin the wheel. Pray for vibes. Cry responsibly.

Scenario 1: Rent is due in 3 days

A) Pay it in full, eat ramen for the rest of the month
B) Pay half, ghost your landlord, block texts
C) Move in with your mom (again) and tell yourself it's "temporary"
D) Apply to another remote job and manifest rent with positive thoughts

Scenario 2: You have $73.42 in your account

A) Gas + groceries = pick one
B) Pretend your student loan autopay doesn't exist
C) Start a GoFundMe called "Help Me Not Be Homeless (Again)"
D) Download four gig apps, delete three after 1 hour

Scenario 3: Utility bill came early

A) Pay just enough to keep the lights dim but dramatic
B) Call and say "I'm experiencing financial hardship" like a script
C) Let it ride, candlelight is romantic
D) Create an Etsy shop called "Unemployed & Unbothered" and sell trauma

Scenario 4: Interview requires business casual

A) Dust off those Target slacks from 2018
B) Thrift store. Pray it doesn't smell like grandma's closet
C) Video call only: rock a blazer + pajama pants combo
D) Sell one of your shoes. Just one. They won't see your feet

Scenario 5: You're out of everything

A) Use the last of your points for an Uber Eats side of fries
B) Visit your friend who always has snacks
C) Go to Costco for free samples, call it lunch
D) Fast. Spiritually and financially.

Bonus Point System:

- +1 point for every bill you paid on time
- +2 points if you didn't cry after opening your bank app
- +3 points if you're still applying to jobs with hope

- +10 points if you somehow still have Wi-Fi

Total 5–15 points? You're a functioning miracle

"What Should I Do About My Bills?"

Subtitle: Screaming into the Void Isn't a Payment Method, I checked.

So you're unemployed (or underpaid), your rent's due, your phone bill is passive-aggressively reminding you it exists, and Sallie Mae is texting you like y'all are friends. Welcome to the financial tightrope known as: "What the hell do I pay first?"

Spoiler: There is no right answer. Only panic math, side hustle fantasies, and a prayer that your cash app balance magically resets overnight.

Let's Break It Down:

Expense	Feeling
Rent	Priority #1, unless your landlord doesn't believe in grace
Utilities	You'll choose between heat and Wi-Fi like a dystopian power move
Phone	Can't job hunt without it, but can you Venmo Verizon? Asking for a friend
Food	Welcome to the "Is it expired or just aged?" diet
Subscriptions	You forgot you still pay for Netflix... whoops
Car Note	Park it in the driveway and call it a "storage fee"
Debt Collectors	They can't take what you don't have, babe. Keep walking

Real Strategies That Aren't Pretty (But Work-ish)

1. Prioritize survival.
   Forget credit score guilt. Pay what keeps you alive and functioning. Food, meds, shelter. Everything else is noise.
2. Negotiate everything.
   Rent? Ask for a delay. Phone? Call customer service. Hospital bill? They've got plans. You'd be surprised what they'll forgive when you sound tired enough.

3. Delete shame.
   You're not bad with money, you're bad with capitalism. There's a difference.
4. Hustle without drowning.
   Gig economy burnout is real. If you're DoorDashing with a cold just to pay off a $34 water bill, pause. You can't help yourself broke, and broken.
5. Check for random aid.
   Mutual aid networks. Local programs. Crowdfunding. That weird Facebook group for struggling professionals. Someone out there might bless you. Or at least PayPal you $20.

Side Hustles That Seem Doable at 2 AM But Rarely Are

- Freelance writing (until they ask for free samples and pay $12/article)
- Selling candles, art, or trauma on Etsy
- Virtual assistant work for someone doing better than you
- Rent-a-friend apps (until someone makes it weird)
- Becoming a "digital creator" and trying not to cry when your reel gets 17 views

Thought Exercise: "If I Had $100 Right Now..."

Do you pay the electric bill?
Buy groceries?
Save it?
Buy a domain name and start your empire?

The fact that you have to think this hard about $100 should be a damn policy issue, not a personal failure.

Affirmation for the Broke, Brilliant, and Barely Hanging On:

I am not my bank account.
I am not my unemployment status.
I am still valuable even when I'm overdrafted.

Final Thought:

Bills don't wait. But neither does your spirit.
You've made it this far with grace, resourcefulness, and a little cussing. That's survival. That's resilience. That's wealth in the making even if your debit card says otherwise right now.

CHAPTER 12

We're Still Here. Somehow.

CHAPTER 12: We're Still Here. Somehow.

You made it through the chapters, and hopefully, through a few breakdowns with your dignity intact. Or maybe not. Either way? You're still here.

In 2025, that alone is a damn achievement.

You've survived being:

- Ignored by recruiters
- Gaslit by job descriptions
- Paid in "team culture"
- Interviewed by 6 people for a job that pays less than your rent
- Told to "pivot," "manifest," or "just network more" by people who've never been laid off a day in their lives

And yet? You're here. Not broken. Just tired. Maybe a little ragey.

But wiser. Sharper. And definitely funnier.

The Job Market Didn't Break You, It Exposed the System

You were never the problem.

The problem is an economy that rewards underpaying talent while glamorizing grind culture.

The problem is AI writing job descriptions, ATS bots rejecting you before a human ever reads your name, and hiring managers asking for 12 years of experience for a junior role.

You did everything "right". school, degrees, internships, staying late, being loyal, and still ended up scrolling job boards like it's your job.

That's not failure. That's a system built to gaslight you.

But Here's What They Can't Take:

They can't take your creativity.
They can't take your lived experience.
They can't take your ability to adapt, show up, or bounce back even when you're hanging on by caffeine and sarcasm.

You may not have a job offer (yet).

You may be budgeting with Monopoly money and emotional coupons.

But you're still standing, and that's not nothing.

What This Book Was (and Wasn't)

This book wasn't about fixing you. You were never broken.

This was a space to say, "Yeah, this sucks, and it's not just me."

It was part therapy, part roast, part handbook, and part rebellion.

Because laughter is survival.
Sarcasm is a weapon.
And honesty? That's power.

A Note from One Job Seeker to Another:

Dear reader, I see you. I am you.
I've cried after rejections.
I've watched the bills stack.
I've wondered if I'm irrelevant, invisible, or just unlucky.

And I've also reminded myself:

"Rejection is redirection."
"Rest isn't laziness."
"And the right role, the right people, the right income will come."

Until then?
We keep applying.
We keep laughing.
We keep living, even if it means doing it between Indeed scrolls and side hustle experiments.

Final Affirmation:

This job market is a circus.
I am not the clown.
I'm the ringmaster... temporarily unemployed, but permanently powerful.

Now close this book, take a deep breath, and do whatever the hell makes you feel alive. You're more than your resume.

You're a f*cking force.

About the Author

Char Vernon is an HR professional, resume whisperer, and unapologetically over it. After 10+ years of the hiring process, I found myself on the other side of the desk, navigating ghosted interviews, lowball offers, and "culture fit" excuses.

I wrote this book not as a career coach, but as a fellow frustrated, qualified, and emotionally unstable job seeker trying to survive the unemployment Olympics.

When I am not dragging the hiring process, I run my own consulting business, write children's books, and occasionally screams into the void.